Steal not this book for fear of shame,
For in it you see the owner's name—
And if I catch you by the tail,
You must prepare for Newgate jail.

Steal not this book for fear of shame,
For in it you see the owner's name—
And if I catch you by the tail,
You must prepare for Newgate jail.

Cakes
and
Custard

CAKES AND CUSTARD

CHILDREN'S RHYMES CHOSEN BY

Brian Alderson

ILLUSTRATED BY

Helen Oxenbury

WILLIAM MORROW AND COMPANY   NEW YORK 1975

Published in the United States in 1975
Text copyright © 1974 by Brian Alderson
Illustrations copyright © 1974 by Helen Oxenbury
Published in Great Britain in 1974

Printed in the United States of America.

1 2 3 4 5 79 78 77 76 75

Library of Congress Catalog Card Number 75-24523

ISBN 0-688-22050-9
ISBN 0-688-32050-3 (lib. bdg.)

Layout and design by Jan Pieńkowski

The editor and illustrator wish to record their gratitude to Mr Robert Graves and Collins-Knowlton-Wing, Inc., for permission to include "Henry and Mary" (from *Collected Poems*) copyright © 1955 Robert Graves, and to Mr James Reeves for permission to include "W" and "Doctor Emmanuel" (from, respectively, *The Blackbird in the Lilac,* London, Oxford University Press, 1952, and *The Wandering Moon,* London, Heinemann, 1957). These original compositions have been placed in the collection in order to show the continuance of the nursery-rhyme tradition in the work of contemporary writers.

WHERE THE RHYMES COME FROM

Most of the rhymes in this collection are traditional to the English nursery or playground. In putting them together I have drawn extensively on printed sources, some of which, like James Orchard Halliwell's *Nursery Rhymes of England*, owed a lot to other printed texts, and some of which, like Norman Douglas's *London Street Games*, recorded the rhymes direct from the children who chanted them. A few rhymes come from childhood recollections – either of my own, or those of friends and relations. I have not scrupled to use unfamiliar variants of common rhymes (like 'Ding Dong Bell') where these may help us to hear afresh what they are saying; nor have I hesitated to make small alterations to words or word-arrangements where these may help the rhythm of the lines. Nursery rhymes are, above all, to be said or sung. The sound that they make is more important than what they look like in print.

B.A.

Girls and boys, come out to play,
The moon doth shine as bright as day;
Leave your supper, and leave your sleep,
And come with your playfellows into the street.
Come with a whoop, come with a call,
Come with a good will or not at all.
Up the ladder and down the wall,
A halfpenny roll will serve us all.
You find milk and I'll find flour,
And we'll have a pudding in half an hour.

How many miles to Babylon?
Threescore miles and ten.
Can I get there by candlelight?
Yes—and back again!
If your heels are nimble and light,
You may get there by candlelight.

The man in the wilderness asked of me,
How many strawberries grew in the sea?
I answered him, as I thought good,
As many red herrings as grew in the wood.

4

When good king Arthur ruled this land,
    He was a goodly king;
He stole three pecks of barley-meal,
    To make a bag-pudding.

A bag-pudding the king did make,
    And stuff'd it well with plums;
And in it put great lumps of fat,
    As big as my two thumbs.

The king and queen did eat thereof,
    And noblemen beside;
And what they could not eat that night,
    The queen next morning fried.

In fir tar is,
In oak none is,
In mud eel is,
In clay none is.
Goat eat ivy,
Mare eat oats.

The man in the moon,
Came tumbling down
And asked his way to Norwich.
He went by the south,
And burnt his mouth
With supping cold pease-porridge.

Sing a song of sixpence,
    A pocket full of rye;
Four and twenty blackbirds
    Baked in a pie;

When the pie was opened
    The birds began to sing;
Wasn't that a dainty dish
    To set before the king?

The king was in his counting house
    Counting out his money;
The queen was in the parlour
    Eating bread and honey;

The maid was in the garden
    Hanging out the clothes,
There came a little blackbird,
    And snapped off her nose.

Jenny was so mad,
    She didn't know what to do;
She put her finger in her ear,
    And cracked it right in two.

One misty moisty morning,
When cloudy was the weather,
There I met an old man
Clothed all in leather;
Clothed all in leather,
With cap under his chin,—
How do you do, and how do you do,
And how do you do again?

There was an old woman toss'd up in a basket
   Nineteen times as high as the moon;
Where she was going I couldn't but ask it,
   For in her hand she carried a broom.

Old woman, old woman, old woman, quoth I,
   O whither, O whither, O whither, so high?
To brush the cobwebs off the sky!
   Shall I go with thee? Aye, by and by.

Awake, arise, pull out your eyes,
    And hear what time of day;
And when you've done, pull out your tongue,
    And see what you can say.

A man of words and not of deeds,
Is like a garden full of weeds;
And when the weeds begin to grow,
It's like a garden full of snow;
And when the snow begins to fall,
It's like a bird upon the wall;
And when the bird away does fly,
It's like an eagle in the sky;
And when the sky begins to roar,
It's like a lion at the door;
And when the door begins to crack,
It's like a stick across your back;
And when your back begins to smart,
It's like a penknife in your heart;
And when your heart begins to bleed,
You're dead, and dead and dead indeed!

Ding, dong, bell,
Pussy's in the well!
Who put her in?—
Little Tommy Lin.
Who pulled her out?—
Dog with long snout.
What a naughty boy was that
To drown poor pussy-cat,
Who never did any harm,
But kill'd the mice in his father's barn.

Tweedle-dum and Tweedle-dee
    Resolved to have a battle,
For Tweedle-dum said Tweedle-dee
    Had spoiled his nice new rattle.
Just then flew by a monstrous crow,
    As big as a tar barrel,
Which frightened both the heroes so,
    They quite forgot their quarrel.

There were three jovial Welshmen,
    As I have heard them say,
And they would go a-hunting
    Upon St David's day.

All the day they hunted,
    And nothing could they find
But a ship a-sailing,
    A-sailing with the wind.

One said it was a ship,
    The other he said, nay;
The third said it was a house,
    With the chimney blown away.

And all the night they hunted,
    And nothing could they find
But the moon a-gliding,
    A-gliding with the wind.

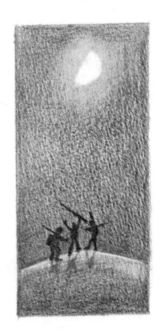

One said it was the moon,
    The other he said, nay;
The third said it was a cheese,
    And half o't cut away.

And all the day they hunted,
    And nothing could they find
But a hedgehog in a bramble bush,
    And that they left behind.

The first said it was a hedgehog,
    The second he said, nay,
The third it was a pincushion,
    And the pins stuck in wrong way.

And all the night they hunted,
    And nothing could they find
But a hare in a turnip field,
    And that they left behind.

The first said it was a hare,
    The second he said, nay,
The third said it was a calf,
    And the cow had run away.

And all the day they hunted,
    And nothing could they find
But an owl in a holly tree,
    And that they left behind.

One said it was an owl,
    The other he said, nay,
The third said it was an old man,
    And his beard growing grey.

Little Polly Flinders
Sat among the cinders
Warming her pretty little toes.
Her mother came and caught her
And whipped her little daughter
For spoiling of her nice new clothes.

There was a jolly miller
Lived on the river Dee,
He look'd upon his pillow,
And there he saw a flea.
    Oh! Mr Flea,
You have been biting me,
And you must die:
    So he crack'd his bones
    Upon the stones,
And there he let him lie.

Don't Care didn't care,
Don't Care was wild,
Don't Care stole plum and pear
Like any beggar's child.

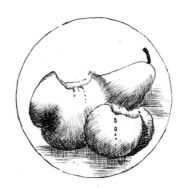

Don't Care was made to care,
Don't Care was hung.
Don't Care was put in a pot
And boiled till he was done.

Little Jack Horner sat in the corner,
    Eating a Christmas pie;
He put in his thumb, and he took out a plum,
    And said, What a good boy am I!

Tom he was a piper's son,
He learn'd to play when he was young,
But all the tunes that he could play,
Was, "Over the hills and far away";
Over the hills, and a great way off,
And the wind will blow my topknot off.

Barber, barber, shave a pig,
How many hairs will make a wig?
"Four and twenty, that's enough,"
Give the barber a pinch of snuff.

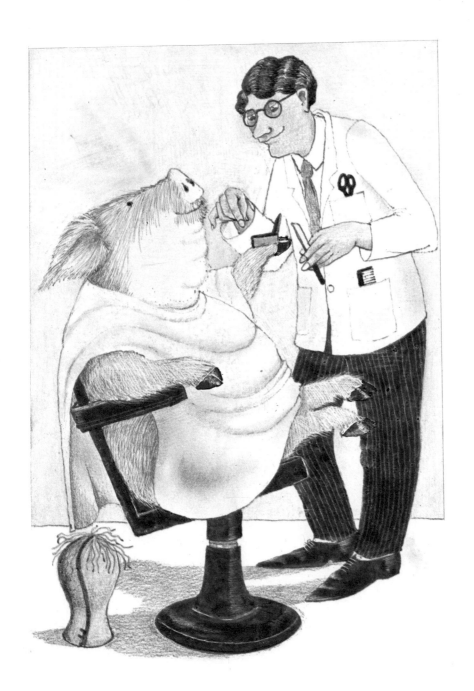

Peter White will ne'er go right.
    Would you know the reason why?
He follows his nose where'er he goes,
    And that stands all awry.

Elsie Marley is grown so fine,
She won't get up to serve the swine,
But lies in bed till eight or nine,
And surely she does take her time.

And do you ken Elsie Marley, honey?
The wife who sells the barley, honey;
She won't get up to serve her swine,
And do you ken Elsie Marley, honey?

Little King Boggen he built a fine hall,
Pie-crust and pastry-crust, that was the wall;
The windows were made of black-puddings and white,
And slated with pancakes—you ne'er saw the like.

Robin the Bobbin, the big-bellied Ben,
He ate more meat than fourscore men;
He ate a cow, he ate a calf,
He ate a butcher and a half;
He ate a church, he ate a steeple,
He ate the priest and all the people.
  A cow and a calf,
  An ox and a half,
  A church and a steeple,
  And all the good people,
And yet he complain'd that his stomach wasn't full.

Solomon Grundy,
Born on a Monday,

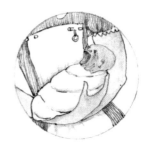

Christened on Tuesday,

Married on Wednesday,

Took ill on Thursday,

Worse on Friday,

Died on Saturday,

Buried on Sunday;

This is the end
Of Solomon Grundy.

Old Abram Brown is dead and gone,
You'll never see him more;
He used to wear a long brown coat,
  That button'd down before.

  Old Sir Simon the king,
And young Sir Simon the squire,
  And old Mrs Hickabout
  Kicked Mrs Kickabout
Round about our coal fire.

Tom, Tom, the piper's son,
Stole a pig, and away he run!
The pig was eat, and Tom was beat,
And he went roaring down the street.

Deedle, deedle, dumpling, my son John
Went to bed with his trousers on;
One shoe off, the other shoe on,
Deedle, deedle, dumpling, my son John.

Taffy was a Welshman, Taffy was a thief,
Taffy came to my house and stole a piece of beef.

I went to Taffy's house, Taffy wasn't home,

Taffy came to my house and stole a marrowbone.

I went to Taffy's house, Taffy wasn't in,

Taffy came to my house and stole a silver pin.

I went to Taffy's house, Taffy was in bed,
I took up a poker and flung it at his head.

Rock-a-bye baby, thy cradle is green;
Father's a nobleman, mother's a queen;
And Betty's a lady, and wears a gold ring;
And Johnny's a drummer, and drums for the king.

Curly locks, curly locks, wilt thou be mine?
Thou shalt not wash dishes, nor yet feed the swine;
But sit on a cushion and sew a fine seam,
And feed upon strawberries, sugar, and cream.

Master I have, and I am his man,
    Gallop a dreary dun;
Master I have, and I am his man,
And I'll get a wife as fast as I can;
With a heighly gaily gamberaily,
    Higgledy piggledy, niggledy, niggledy,
    Gallop a dreary dun.

I had a young man,
He was double-jointed,
When I kissed him,
He was disappointed.

When he died
I had another one,
God bless his little heart,
I found a better one.

If you sneeze on Monday, you sneeze for danger;
Sneeze on a Tuesday, kiss a stranger;
Sneeze on a Wednesday, sneeze for a letter;
Sneeze on a Thursday, something better;
Sneeze on a Friday, sneeze for sorrow;
Sneeze on a Saturday, see your sweetheart tomorrow.

See this pretty little girl of mine,
She brought me a penny and a bottle of wine.
A bottle of wine and a penny too,
See what my little girl can do.

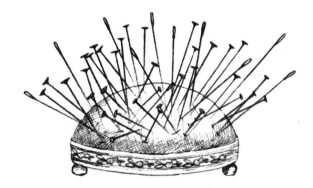

Needles and pins, needles and pins,
When a man marries his trouble begins.

Eight o'clock is striking,
Mother may I go out?
My young man is waiting
To take me round about.

First he gave me apples,
Then he gave me pears;
Then he gave me sixpence
To kiss him on the stairs.

42

Half a pound of bacon,
    Fry it in the pan—
No one else shall have it,
    But me and my young man.

Tommy Trot, a man of law,
Sold his bed and lay upon straw:
Sold the straw and slept on grass,
To buy his wife a looking-glass.

Eaper Weaper, chimbley sweeper,
Had a wife but couldn't keep her;
Had anovver, didn't love her,
Up the chimbley he did shove her.

As I was going up the hill,
    I met with Jack the piper,
And all the tunes that he could play
    Was "Tie up your petticoats tighter."
I tied them once, I tied them twice,
    I tied them three times over;
And all the songs that he could sing
    Was "Carry me safe to Dover."

I saw a ship a-sailing
  A-sailing on the sea;
And, oh! it was all laden
  With pretty things for thee!

There were comfits in the cabin,
  And apples in the hold;
The sails were made of silk,
  And the masts were made of gold:

The four-and-twenty sailors
  That stood between the decks
Were four-and-twenty white mice,
  With chains about their necks.

The captain was a duck,
  With a packet on his back;
And when the ship began to move,
  The captain said, "Quack! quack!"

I had a little husband,
    No bigger than my thumb,
I put him in a pint pot,
    And there I bid him drum.

I bought a little horse,
    That galloped up and down;
I bridled him, and saddled him,
    And sent him out of town.

I gave him some garters,
    To garter up his hose,
And a little handkerchief,
    To wipe his pretty nose.

48

As I was going up Pippen-hill,
    Pippen-hill was dirty,
There I met a pretty miss,
    And she dropped me a curtsey.

Little miss, pretty miss,
    Blessings light upon you!
If I had half-a-crown a day,
    I'd spend it all upon you.

Saw ye aught of my love a-coming from ye market?
A pack of meal upon her back,
A baby in her basket;
Saw ye aught of my love a-coming from ye market?

Brave news is come to town,
Brave news is carried;
Brave news is come to town,
Jemmy Dawson's married.

Birds of a feather flock together,
    And so will pigs and swine;
Rats and mice will have their choice,
    And so will I have mine.

Young Roger came tapping at Dolly's window,
Thumpetty, thumpetty, thump!
He asked for admittance, she answered him "No!"
Frumpetty, frumpetty, frump!

The fair maid who, the first of May,
Goes to the fields at break of day,
And washes in dew from the hawthorn tree,
Will ever after handsome be.

On Saturday night
Shall be all my care,
To powder my locks
And curl my hair.

On Sunday morning
My love will come in,
When he will marry me
With a gold ring.

Henry was a young king,
Mary was his queen;
He gave her a snowdrop
On a stalk of green.

Then all for his kindness
And all for his care
She gave him a new-laid egg
In the garden there.

"Love can you sing?"—"I cannot sing."
"Or tell a tale?"—"Not one I know."
"Then let us play at queen and king
As down the garden walks we go."

Little Tom Tucker
Sings for his supper;
What shall he eat?
White bread and butter.
How shall he cut it
Without e'er a knife?
How will he be married
Without e'er a wife?

56

What are little boys made of, made of,
What are little boys made of?
Snaps and snails and puppy-dogs' tails;
And that's what little boys are made of, made of.

What are little girls made of, made of,
What are little girls made of?
Sugar and spice, and all that's nice;
And that's what little girls are made of, made of.

Come, let's to bed,
Says Sleepy-head;
Tarry a while, says Slow:

Put on the pot,
Says Greedy-gut,
Let's sup before we go.

Oh! mother, I shall be married to Mr Punchinello.
    To Mr Punch,
    To Mr Joe,
    To Mr Nell,
    To Mr Lo,
    Mr Punch, Mr Joe,
    Mr Nell, Mr Lo,
    To Mr Punchinello.

If all the food was paving-stones,
And all the seas were ink,
What would we poor mortals do
For victuals and for drink?

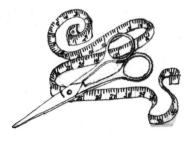

Bounce Buckram, velvet's dear;
Christmas comes but once a year.

The north wind doth blow,
And we shall have snow,
And what will poor Robin do then?
Poor thing!
He'll sit in a barn,
And to keep himself warm,
Will hide his head under his wing.
Poor thing!

I had a little nut-tree, nothing would it bear
But a silver nutmeg and a golden pear;
The king of Spain's daughter came to visit me,
And all was because of my little nut-tree.
I skipp'd over water, I danced over sea,
And all the birds in the air couldn't catch me.

Please to remember
The fifth of November,
    Gunpowder treason and plot;
I know no reason
Why gunpowder treason
    Should ever be forgot.

William and Mary, George and Anne,
Four such children had never a man:
They put their father to flight and shame,
And called their brother a shocking bad name.

High diddle ding,
Did you hear the bells ring?
The parliament soldiers are gone to the king!
Some they did laugh, some they did cry,
To see the parliament soldiers pass by.

Daffy-down-dilly has come up to town,
In a yellow petticoat, and a green gown.

O the cuckoo she's a pretty bird,
    She singeth as she flies,
She bringeth good tidings,
    She telleth no lies.

She sucketh white flowers
    For to keep her voice clear,
And the more she singeth cuckoo
    The summer draweth near.

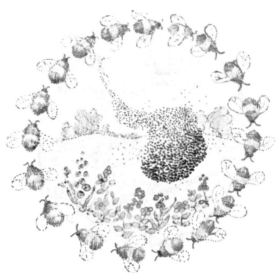

A swarm of bees in May
Is worth a load of hay;

A swarm of bees in June
Is worth a silver spoon;

A swarm of bees in July
Is not worth a fly.

There was a piper, he'd a cow;
    And he'd no hay to give her;
He took his pipes and played a tune,
    Consider, old cow, consider!

The cow considered very well,
    For she gave the piper a penny,
That he might play the tune again,
    Of corn rigs are bonnie!

I had a little pony,
　　His name was Dapple Grey,
I sent him to a lady,
　　To ride a mile away.
She whipped him, she slashed him,
　　She rode him through the mire;
I would not lend my pony now
　　For all the lady's hire.

Baa, baa, black sheep,
    Have you any wool?
Yes, marry, have I,
    Three bags full:

One for my master,
    And one for my dame,
But none for the little boy
    Who cries in the lane.

Grandpa Grig had a pig
In a field of clover;
Piggie died, Grandpa cried,
And all the fun was over.

Hickety, pickety, my black hen,
She lays eggs for gentlemen;
Gentlemen come every day,
To see what my black hen doth lay.

The Cock Lock the dairy door,
           Lock the dairy door!

The Hen Chickle, chackle, chee,
           I haven't got the key!

There was a monkey climb'd up a tree,
When he fell down, then down fell he.

There was a crow sat on a stone,
When he was gone, then there was none.

There was an old wife did eat an apple,
When she had eat two, she had eat a couple.

There was a horse going to the mill,
When he went on, he stood not still.

There was a butcher cut his thumb,
When it did bleed, then blood did come.

There was a lackey ran a race,
When he ran fast, he ran apace.

There was a cobbler clouting shoon,
When they were mended, they were done.

There was a chandler making candle,
When he them stripped, he did them handle.

There was a navy went into Spain,
When it return'd it came again.

Incey Wincey Spider
Climbed the water spout.
Down came the rain
And washed poor Wincey out.
Out came the sun
And dried up all the rain,
So Incey Wincey Spider
Climbed the spout again.

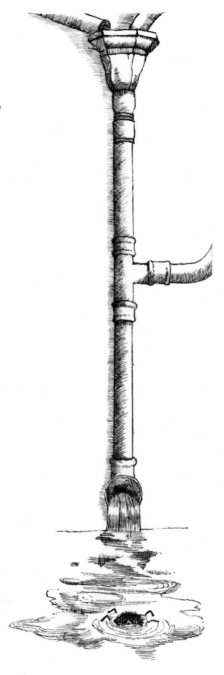

Ladybird, ladybird, fly away home,
Thy house is on fire, thy children all gone,
All but one, and her name is Ann,
And she crept under the pudding-pan.

The cat sat asleep by the side of the fire,
  The mistress snored loud as a pig:
Jack took up his fiddle, by Jenny's desire,
  And struck up a bit of a jig.

Goosey, goosey, gander,
   Where shall I wander?
Up stairs, down stairs,
   And in my lady's chamber:
There I met an old man
   That would not say his prayers;
I took him by the left leg,
   And threw him down stairs.

81

There was an old woman sat spinning,
And that's the first beginning;
    She had a calf,
    And that's half,
She took it by the tail,
And threw it over the wall,
And that's all.

There was a man, and he had nought,
    And robbers came to rob him;
He crept up to the chimney pot,
    And then they thought they had him.

But he got down on t'other side,
    And then they could not find him;
He ran fourteen miles in fifteen days,
    And never looked behind him.

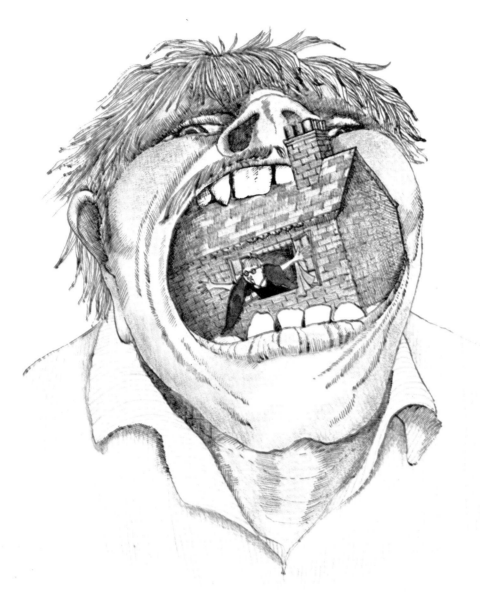

There was an old woman called Nothing-at-all,
Who rejoiced in a dwelling exceedingly small:
A man stretched his mouth to its utmost extent,
And down at one gulp house and old woman went.

Hannah Bantry in the pantry,
    Eating of a mutton-bone;
How she gnawed it, how she clawed it,
    When she found she was alone!

Jack and Jill went up the hill,
   To fetch a pail of water;
Jack fell down and broke his crown,
   And Jill came tumbling after.

I'll tell you a story
    About Jack-a-Nory—
And now my story's begun:
    I'll tell you another
    About Jack and his brother—
And now my story's done.

There was an old woman, her name it was Peg;
Her head was of wood, and she wore a cork leg.
The neighbours all pitched her into the water,
Her leg was drowned first, and her head followed a'ter.

Hey! diddle, diddle,
The cat and the fiddle,
The cow jumped over the moon;
The little dog laughed
To see the sport,
While the dish ran after the spoon.

Gay go up, and gay go down,
To ring the bells of London town.

Bull's eyes and targets,
Say the bells of St Marg'ret's.

Brickbats and tiles,
Say the bells of St Giles'.

Halfpence and farthings,
Say the bells of St Martin's.

Oranges and lemons,
Say the bells of St Clement's.

Pancakes and fritters,
Say the bells of St Peter's.

Two sticks and an apple,
Say the bells at Whitechapel.

Old Father Baldpate,
Say the slow bells at Aldgate.

You owe me ten shillings,
Say the bells at St Helen's.

Pokers and tongs,
Say the bells at St John's.

Kettles and pans,
Say the bells at St Ann's.

When will you pay me?
Say the bells at Old Bailey.

When I grow rich,
Say the bells at Shoreditch.

Pray when will that be?
Say the bells at Stepney.

I'm sure I don't know,
Says the great bell at Bow.

Here comes a candle to light you to bed,
And here comes a chopper to chop off your head.

We're all in the dumps,
　　For diamonds are trumps;
The kittens are gone to St Paul's!
　　The babies are bit,
　　The moon's in a fit,
And the houses are built without walls.

Little girl, little girl, where have you been?
Gathering roses to give to the queen.
Little girl, little girl, what gave she you?
She gave me a diamond as big as my shoe.

Pussy-cat, pussy-cat, where have you been?
I've been up to London to look at the queen.
Pussy-cat, pussy-cat, what did you there?
I frightened a little mouse under the chair.

There was an old woman who lived in a shoe,
She had so many children she didn't know what to do;
She gave them some broth without any bread,
She whipped them all well and put them to bed.

Little Tommy Tittlemouse
Lived in a little house;

He caught fishes
In others men's ditches.

Sally go round the sun;

Sally go round the moon;

Sally go round the omnibus
On a Saturday afternoon.

Jack, Jack, the bread's a-burning,
    All to a cinder.
If you don't come and fetch it out,
    We'll throw it through the winder.

Tell tale, tit!
Your tongue shall be slit,
And all the dogs in the town
Shall have a little bit.

Policeman, policeman, don't take me!
Take that man behind that tree!
I stole brass, he stole gold.
Policeman, policeman, don't take hold!

Who comes here?
  A grenadier.
What do you want?
  A pot of beer.
Where's your money?
  I've forgot.
Then get you gone
  You drunken sot!

Desperate Dan
The dirty old man
Washed his face
In a frying-pan;
Combed his hair
With the leg of a chair;
Desperate Dan
The dirty old man.

House to let,
Rent to pay,
Knock at the door
And run away.

Up and down Pie Street,
    The windows made of glass,
Call at Number Thirty-three,
    You'll see a pretty lass.

Her name is Annie Robinson,
    Catch her if you can,
She married Charlie Anderson,
    Before he was a man.

Bread and dripping all the week,
    Pig's head on Sunday,
Half a crown on Saturday night,
    A farthing left for Monday.

She only bought a bonnet-box,
    He only bought a ladle,
So when the little baby came
    It hadn't got no cradle.

Margery Mutton-pie and Johnny Bopeep,
They met together in Gracechurch Street;
In and out, in and out, over the way,
Oh! says Johnny, 'tis chop-nose day.

If I'd as much money as I could spend,
I never would cry old chairs to mend;
Old chairs to mend, old chairs to mend;
I never would cry old chairs to mend.

If I'd as much money as I could tell,
I never would cry old clothes to sell;
Old clothes to sell, old clothes to sell;
I never would cry old clothes to sell.

I am a little beggar girl,
My mother she is dead,
My father is a drunkard
And won't give me no bread.
I look out of the window
To hear the organ play—
God bless my dear mother,
She's gone far away.

Here am I, little jumping Joan;
When nobody's with me
I'm always alone.

When Jacky's a very good boy,
    He shall have cakes and custard;
When he does nothing but cry,
    He shall have nothing but mustard.

Old Mother Roundabout
Knocking all the kids about
Outside Elsie's door.
Up comes Elsie with a great big stick
And lets her know what for.

Piggy on the railway
Picking up stones,
Along came an engine
And broke Piggy's bones.

"Oy," said Piggy,
"That's not fair."
"Pooh," said the engine-driver,
"I don't care."

My mother said
I never should
Play with the gypsies
In the wood.
If I did,
She would say,
Naughty girl to disobey.
Your hair shan't curl
And your shoes shan't shine,
You gypsy girl
You shan't be mine.
My father said
That if I did
He'd rap my head with the teapot lid.

The wood was dark, the grass was green
Along came Sally with a tambourine.
I went to sea—no ship to get across,
I paid ten shillings for a blind white horse.
I up on his back
And was off in a crack,
Sally tell my mother that I shan't come back.

Pease-pudding hot,
    Pease-pudding cold,
Pease-pudding in the pot,
    Nine days old.
Some like it hot,
    Some like it cold,
Some like it in the pot,
    Nine days old.

Well I never,
Did you ever
See a monkey
Dressed in leather?
Leather eyes,
Leather nose,
Leather buttons
To his toes.

As I went over the water,
The water went over me,
I saw two little blackbirds sitting on a tree:
The one called me a rascal,
The other called me thief;
I took up my little black stick,
And knocked out all their teeth.

Poor old Robinson Crusoe!
Poor old Robinson Crusoe!
They made him a coat
Of an old nanny goat,
    I wonder how they could do so!
With a ring a ting tang,
With a ring a ting tang,
    Poor old Robinson Crusoe!

Roley Poley, pudding and pie,
Kissed the girls and made them cry;
When the boys came out to play,
Roley Poley ran away.

120

Oh dear me! Mother caught a flea;
Put it in the teapot to make a cup of tea.

Bow, wow, wow,
    Whose dog art thou?
Little Tom Tinker's dog,
    Bow, wow, wow.

There was a crooked man,
and he went a crooked mile,

He found a crooked sixpence
against a crooked stile:

He bought a crooked cat,
which caught a crooked mouse,

And they all lived together
in a little crooked house.

Last night and the night before
Twenty-five robbers knocked at the door.
Johnny got up to let them in
And hit them on the head with a rolling pin.

Dickery, dickery, dare,
The pig flew up in the air;
The man in brown soon brought him down,
Dickery, dickery, dare.

The lion and the unicorn
    Were fighting for the crown;
The lion beat the unicorn
    All round the town.
Some gave them white bread,
    And some gave them brown;
Some gave them plum-cake,
    And sent them out of town.

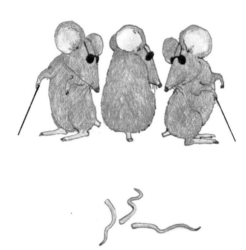

Three blind mice, see how they run!
They all ran after the farmer's wife,
Who cut off their tails with the carving-knife,
Did ever you see such fools in your life?
               Three blind mice.

Ride a cock-horse to Banbury cross,
To see a young lady upon a white horse,
Rings on her fingers, and bells on her toes,
And so she makes music wherever she goes.

To market, to market, to buy a fat pig,
　　Home again, home again, dancing a jig;
Ride to market to buy a fat hog,
　　Home again, home again, jiggety-jog.

A cat came fiddling out of a barn,
With a pair of bagpipes under her arm;
She could sing nothing but fiddle cum fee,
The mouse has married the humble-bee.
Pipe, cat; dance, mouse,
We'll have a wedding at our good house.

To market, to market, a gallop, a trot,
To buy some meat to put in the pot;
Threepence a quarter, a groat a side,
If it hadn't been killed, it must have died.

A diller, a dollar,
A ten o'clock scholar,
What makes you come so soon?
You used to come at ten o'clock,
But now you come at noon.

Doctor Emmanuel Harrison–Hyde
Has a very big head with brains inside.
I wonder what happens inside the brains
That Doctor Emmanuel's head contains?

As Tommy Snooks and Bessy Brooks
Were walking out one Sunday,
Says Tommy Snooks to Bessy Brooks,
"Tomorrow will be Monday."

Jack Sprat could eat no fat,
   His wife could eat no lean;
And so, betwixt them both, you see,
   They licked the platter clean.

One, two,
Buckle my shoe;

Three, four,
Shut the door;

Five, six,
Pick up sticks;

Seven, eight,
Lay them straight;

Nine, ten,
A good fat hen;

Eleven, twelve,
Who will delve;

Thirteen, fourteen,
Maids a-courting;

Fifteen, sixteen,
Maids a-kissing;

Seventeen, eighteen,
Maids a-waiting;

Nineteen, twenty,
My stomach's empty.

A, B, C, tumble down D,
The cat's in the cupboard and can't see me.

Apple-pie, pudding and pancake,
All begins with an A.

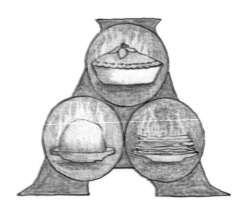

1, 2, 3, 4, 5!
I caught a hare alive;
6, 7, 8, 9, 10!
I let her go again.

Twelve huntsmen with horns and hounds,
Hunting over other men's grounds.

Eleven ships sailing o'er the main,
Some bound for France and some for Spain:
I wish them all safe home again:

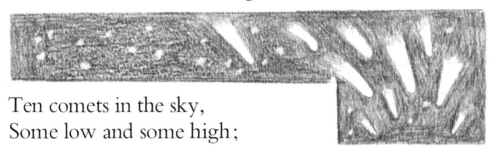

Ten comets in the sky,
Some low and some high;

Nine peacocks in the air,
I wonder how they all come there,
I do not know, and do not care;

Eight joiners in joiner's hall,
Working with the tools and all;

Seven lobsters in a dish,
As fresh as any heart could wish;

Six beetles against the wall,
Close by an old woman's apple stall;

Five puppies of our dog Ball,
Who daily for their breakfast call;

Four horses stuck in a bog,

Three monkeys tied to a clog;

Two pudding-ends would choke a dog,

With a gaping, wide-mouthed, waddling frog.

The king sent for his wise men all
    To find a rhyme for W;
When they had thought a good long time
But could not think of a single rhyme,
    "I'm sorry," said he, "to trouble you."

One-ery, two-ery,
    Ziccary zan;
Hollow bone, crack a bone,
    Nine-ery, ten;
Spittery spot,
    It must be done;
Twiddleum twaddleum,
    Twenty-one.

Hink spink, the puddings stink,
    The fat begins to fry,
No one at home, but jumping Joan,
    Father, mother and I.
Stick, stock, stone dead,
    Blind man can't see,
Every knave will have a slave,
    You or I must be he.

Penny on the water,
Tuppence on the sea,
Threepence on the railway,
Out goes she.

I-N spells in—
I was in my kitchen
Doing a bit of stitching,
Old Father Nimble
Came and took my thimble,
I got up a great big stone,
Hit him on the belly bone—
O-U-T spells out.

Adam and Eve and Pinch-me-tight
Went down to the river to bathe.
Adam and Eve were drowned,
Who do you think was saved?

What's the news of the day,
Good neighbour, I pray?
They say the balloon
Is gone up to the moon.

Feedum, fiddledum, fee,
The cat's got into the tree,
    Pussy, come down,
      Or I'll crack your crown,
And toss you into the sea.

Baby and I
    Were baked in a pie,
The gravy was wonderful hot:
    We had nothing to pay
    To the baker that day,
And so we crept out of the pot.

The barber shaved the mason,
    As I suppose
    Cut off his nose,
And popped it in the bason.

146

There was a man of Newington,
    And he was wond'rous wise,
He jumped into a quickset hedge,
    And scratched out both his eyes:
But when he saw his eyes were out,
    With all his might and main
He jump'd into another hedge,
    And scratch'd 'em in again.

Three children sliding on the ice
    Upon a summer's day,
As it fell out, they all fell in,
    The rest they ran away.

Now had these children been at home,
    Or sliding on dry ground,
Ten thousand pounds to one penny
    They had not all been drowned.

You parents all that children have,
    And you that have got none,
If you would have them safe abroad,
    Pray keep them safe at home.

Hector Protector was dressed all in green;
Hector Protector was sent to the Queen.
The Queen did not like him,
Nor more did the King:
So Hector Protector was sent back again.

Trip upon trenchers, and dance upon dishes,
My mother sent me for some barm, some barm;

She bid me tread lightly, and come again quickly,
For fear the young men should do me some harm.

Yet didn't you see, yet didn't you see,
What naughty tricks they put upon me:

They broke my pitcher,
    And spilt the water,
And huffed my mother,
    And chid her daughter,

And kissed my sister instead of me.

Three wise men of Gotham
Went to sea in a bowl:
And if the bowl had been stronger,
My song would have been longer.

If wishes were horses,
    Beggars would ride;
If turnips were watches,
    I'd wear one by my side.

Go to bed first, a golden purse;
Go to bed second, a golden pheasant;
Go to bed third, a golden bird!

Gray goose and gander
    Waft your wings together,
And carry the good king's daughter
    Over the one strand river.

154

Rosemary green,
And lavender blue,
Thyme and sweet marjoram,
Hyssop and rue.

The rose is red, the grass is green,
The days are spent which I have seen,
When I am dead then ring my knell,
And take my book and use him well.

INDEX OF FIRST LINES

F for fig, *I* for jig
N for knuckle bones,
I for John the waterman,
And *S* for sack of stones.

F for fig, *I* for jig
N for knuckle bones,
I for John the waterman,
And *S* for sack of stones.